Publishing Made Easy

A Step-By-Step Guide To
Successful Book Publishing

**Kyra Schaefer, CEO
As You Wish Publishing**

Copyright © 2025 by Kyra Schaefer

All rights reserved.

ISBN: 978-1-951131-77-7

No portion of this book may be reproduced in any form without written permission from the publisher or author, except as permitted by U.S. copyright law.

Contents

Introduction	V
The As You Wish Publishing Way	VII
1. Preparing Your Manuscript for Publishing	1
2. Using AI as an Assistant not a Replacement	11
3. Types of Books Authors Can Publish	17
4. Understanding Publishing Platforms	27
5. Step-by-Step Guide to Publishing with KDP	35
6. Step-by-Step Guide to Publishing with IngramSpark	45
7. Step-by-Step Guide to Publishing with Draft2Digital	53
8. Creating Audiobooks with Audible (ACX)	59
9. Setting Up a Publisher Imprint	67
10. Starting Your Publishing Business	75

11. Marketing Your Book	83
12. Post-Publication Strategies	103
13. Long-Term Success in Publishing	111
Conclusion	123
Appendices	125
About the author	135

Introduction

Welcome to *Publishing Made Easy: Your Step-By-Step Guide to Successful Book Publishing*! This book is designed to empower you with the knowledge and tools needed to publish your book and navigate the world of self-publishing with confidence and clarity. Whether you're a first-time author, an entrepreneur looking to establish a publishing business, or a seasoned writer aiming to refine your approach, this guide offers actionable insights tailored to your needs.

In today's dynamic publishing landscape, authors have more opportunities than ever to take control of their creative works. From formatting your manuscript and designing an eye-catching cover to leveraging publishing platforms like KDP, IngramSpark, and Draft2Digital, this guide walks you through every step of the process. We'll also explore strategies for creating audiobooks, setting up a publisher imprint, and even establishing your own publishing business.

By the end of this guide, you will:

- Understand the full scope of the publishing process, from manuscript preparation to post-launch strategies.

- Learn the step-by-step instructions for publishing on key platforms, ensuring your book reaches its intended audience.

- Gain insights into the technical aspects of publishing, such as obtaining ISBNs, applying for a Library of Congress Control Number, and choosing the right distribution channels.

- Discover marketing techniques to maximize your book's visibility and sales.

Publishing your book is a journey, and this guide serves as your roadmap. Let's get started on turning your publishing dreams into reality.

The As You Wish Publishing Way

Why We Became Publishers

A close friend of mine, who was deeply involved in collaboration books and summits, tragically passed away in a car accident. She was a self-help enthusiast—vibrant, excitable, and full of joy. She had her ups and downs, as we all do, but she was always incredibly supportive, uplifting, and positive. Her sudden death was absolutely devastating to our community.

At the time, I was running something called the Holistic Speakers Guild. It was a group where we held summits, speaking engagements, and meetings. Before her passing, I had been encouraging her to do more—make videos, speak her truth, and put herself out there. Ironically, one of the last videos she made, which I had pushed her to do, was later featured on the evening news when they reported her death. In that video, she spoke about love—loving ourselves and each other. It was hauntingly prophetic.

After her passing, our grieving group felt a strong pull to honor her memory. It felt like a calling. On November 7th, 2017, at 7:00 a.m., I had a moment of lightning-bolt inspiration. I went online and posted: *Who wants to write a book with me?*

Initially, I didn't get much encouragement. People doubted my abilities—and honestly, I didn't know what I was doing. But thankfully, someone in the group, Shanda Trofe, whom my late friend had tried to connect me with earlier, stepped in. Shanda knew how to publish books and offered to teach me.

From there, my journey began. Instead of just publishing my own book, I realized there were many others who wanted to publish but might not have a full book in them or the resources to produce a solo book. Collaboration books offered a more accessible option.

However, it wasn't an easy road. It took me a full year to publish my first collaboration book because I had a limiting belief that once the book was published, my grieving process had to be over. That wasn't true. It was just fear holding me back. When I finally published, it felt both honoring and incredibly challenging.

The process itself was full of obstacles. Getting contributors to meet deadlines, formatting the book in long-form Word documents, figuring out headers, footers, mirrored indents, drop caps, and page numbers—it all took days, even weeks. Adding bios, images, and handling the variety of contributions was overwhelming. Then there was the cover design, which had to satisfy everyone, and selecting the right title, which was another major challenge.

Once the book was ready, I faced the hurdles of launching. I made the mistake of trying to coordinate the launch while out of town, thinking I could enjoy the process. It was anything but enjoyable—I couldn't sleep, the categories on Amazon weren't updating, and reviews weren't coming in as expected. I didn't fully understand the intricacies of Amazon's algorithms, bestseller strategies, and category selection. Thankfully, I avoided some major mistakes by double-checking things with my mentor, but the experience was exhausting.

Despite all this, the book became an Amazon bestseller. Yet, even after publication, the feedback was overwhelming—everyone had an opinion about the cover, the content, and the process. It was a lesson in staying true to my vision and trusting my instincts.

Publishing your first book—whether a collaboration or solo effort—is a monumental task. It's crucial to be clear about your goals, ensure your book is properly formatted and copyedited, and choose a marketable cover design. Picking the right categories, getting your book on platforms like IngramSpark, and reaching out to independent bookstores are all important steps.

Most importantly, don't stop at just one book. Your first book is a foundation. It's intellectual property (IP) you can expand on, not just a bucket-list item to check off. This book—and the ones that follow—are part of a larger vision. Commit to understanding the process, use this book and future resources to refine your skills, and keep building on what you've created.

At As You Wish (AYW) Publishing, we've refined a unique and effective system to guide authors from concept to publication, producing hundreds of successful authors. This "secret sauce" is built on clarity, structure, and support. Whether you're looking to publish a solo project or collaborate with others in a themed anthology, this guide will help you replicate our results.

The Flex System: Effortless Publishing

Our Flex System is designed for ease and efficiency, offering authors a clear roadmap to publication. Here's how it works:

1. **Choose Your Package**

Select the publishing option that aligns with your goals. The Flex System provides scalable enhancements, including options for formatting, book cover design, and more.

2. **Submission Timeline**
Authors have up to two years from purchase to submit their manuscript to our team. This flexibility ensures you have the time needed to perfect your work.

3. **Professional Formatting and Final Approvals**
Once your manuscript is submitted, our team takes over. We:

    - Format your book for both print and digital platforms.

    - Collaborate with you to finalize the book cover design.

    - Conduct final approval checks to set your book up for success.

4. **Speed to Market**
Your paperback and eBook are typically published within 90 days of manuscript submission. This rapid timeline ensures your work reaches readers quickly and efficiently.

The Collaboration Method: Creating Magic Together

Collaboration books are a hallmark of AYW Publishing, fostering community and amplifying voices. Books like *Guided by Spirit* and *Awaken Your Magic* showcase the power of shared storytelling. Here's how we bring these projects to life:

1. **Concept Development**

   - We develop a compelling theme and title.
   - Create a professional book cover design to set the tone and attract contributors.
   - Launch targeted marketing to recruit contributors.

2. **Step-by-Step Process for Contributors**

   Pre-Step 1: Audio Transcription (Optional)

Key Elements of the AYW Secret Sauce

1. **Clear Communication**

   - We provide contributors with detailed, step-by-step guidance to ensure a seamless experience.

2. **Efficient Systems**

- From submission portals to templates, our tools streamline the process for authors and contributors alike.

3. **Community Support**

   - Private Facebook groups foster collaboration, support, and accountability among authors.

4. **Focus on Professionalism**

   - High-quality design, editing, and formatting ensure books meet industry standards.

5. **Launch Strategy**

   - Structured launch plans maximize visibility and reader engagement, leveraging ARC copies, reviews, and social media buzz.

Recreating Our Results

By following these principles and processes, you can replicate the success of AYW Publishing. Whether publishing your own solo book or spearheading a collaboration project, our method provides a proven framework for impactful and efficient publishing.

> "WRITING A BOOK IS AN ADVENTURE. PUBLISHING IT IS A REVOLUTION."
>
> ―――
>
> *Unknown*

Chapter 1

Preparing Your Manuscript for Publishing

Publishing success starts with a strong foundation: a polished and professional manuscript. In this chapter, we'll cover everything you need to know about preparing your manuscript for publishing.

Importance of Editing and Proofreading

- **Hiring Professional Editors:** Professional editors play a vital role in transforming your manuscript into a polished, reader-ready product. Editors bring an objective perspective, catching inconsistencies, errors, and gaps in your narrative that you might overlook. Whether it's refining the overall structure with a developmental editor or ensuring grammar accuracy with a proofreader, their expertise can elevate your book's quality. Platforms like Reedsy, Upwork, and Fiverr provide access to a diverse range of editors who can suit your needs and budget. Investing in professional editing is an investment in your readers' satisfaction.

- **Tools for Self-Editing:** Self-editing is an essential step before hiring a professional editor. It not only helps reduce the cost of editing but also ensures you're presenting the best version of your manuscript. Tools like Grammarly and ProWritingAid are invaluable for catching grammatical errors, improving sentence structure, and enhancing readability. To make the most of self-editing, work in focused rounds—first addressing content and structure, then grammar and style, and finally typos. Reading your manuscript aloud can also reveal awkward phrasing or inconsistencies in tone.

Formatting Your Manuscript

- **Formatting for Print:** Proper formatting is crucial for creating a professional-looking print book. Tools like Atticus (Windows and Mac-friendly) and Vellum (Mac-only) simplify the process, offering user-friendly templates and customization options. Key formatting elements include choosing appropriate margins, font sizes, and line spacing to ensure readability and adherence to industry standards. For those on a budget, online tutorials and free templates can guide you through the DIY process. Regardless of your approach, prioritize creating a layout that enhances the reader's experience.

- **Formatting for eBooks:** Digital formats like ePub and MOBI are essential for eBooks, enabling compatibility with popular devices like Kindle and Nook. Tools like Calibre and Draft2Digital's free formatting service make it easy to convert your manuscript into these formats. Pay attention to font choices, spacing, and hyperlinking chapters for seamless navigation. Testing your eBook on various devices ensures that your readers enjoy a consistent experience regardless of their preferred platform.

Cover Design

- **Hiring a Designer:** Your book's cover is its first impression, making it a critical factor in attracting readers. A professional designer can craft a visually appealing cover that aligns with your book's genre and audience expectations. Platforms like Fiverr, 99designs, and Behance connect you with experienced designers who can bring your vision to life. A well-designed cover not only conveys professionalism but also boosts your book's marketability, helping it stand out in a crowded marketplace.

- **DIY Design Options:** If hiring a designer isn't feasible, tools like Canva and Book Brush empower you to create your own cover with ease. These platforms offer pre-designed templates tailored for book covers, allowing customization to fit your title, genre, and brand. While designing your cover, ensure it adheres to platform specifications such as resolution and size. Striking the right balance between creativity and professionalism can make your DIY cover just as impactful as one designed by a pro.

By following these steps, you'll have a well-polished manuscript and a professionally formatted book that's ready for publishing. Next, we'll explore the publishing platforms available to bring your book to market.

Pitfalls: Preparing Your Manuscript for Publishing

When preparing your manuscript for publishing, it's crucial to avoid some common pitfalls.

1. Skipping Professional Editing and Proofreading

One of the biggest mistakes authors make is choosing not to invest in professional editing or proofreading. Even if you're a skilled writer—or even a copyeditor—it's invaluable to have a third party with a discerning eye review your work. This should be someone trustworthy, supportive, and experienced enough to provide constructive feedback. They can catch things you might overlook, identify areas that fall flat, or highlight sections that might confuse your readers.

While this can be a friend with a good eye, it's often worth hiring a professional. Think of it this way: even though you're self-publishing, that doesn't mean you shouldn't outsource where needed. For example, I hire an accountant because I don't want to learn accounting or risk messing it up. Similarly, hiring an editor or proofreader ensures your book is polished and professional.

2. Overlooking Professional Formatting

The way your book looks on the page matters more than most authors realize. It's about the reader's experience. Some authors think, "I wrote a great book; the content speaks for itself." But presentation is critical.

Imagine going to a restaurant and ordering spaghetti, only to receive a deconstructed mess—noodles on one side, sauce splashed across the plate, parmesan on another dish entirely. That's how an unformatted book feels to readers. Instead, your book should be a cohesive, well-structured experience, consistent and uniform throughout.

This includes interior fonts, which should align with the tone of your book and may even complement the fonts on your cover. Programs like Atticus or Vellum can help you automate and elevate your formatting, creating a polished, professional look.

3. Ignoring the Importance of Cover Design

Your book's cover is its first impression, and while we all have personal preferences, creating a marketable design often requires professional help. A good designer understands trends, how colors work together (or clash), and how to use white space effectively. They can also ensure your cover isn't too busy or overwhelming.

Even if you're learning design tools like Canva or studying design principles, having a professional designer can make a huge difference. They bring an objective perspective and expertise that elevates your book. I've learned a lot about formatting and cover design over the years, but I still hire designers because I know enough to recognize what I don't know.

4. Underestimating the Learning Curve

While you can (and should) learn as much as you can about publishing tools and resources, it's also important to recognize that this is a continuous journey.

Tools like Atticus, Grammarly, and Canva are excellent investments, but they often come with a cost—both in terms of money and time to learn.

When I teach publishing courses, I recommend these tools because they can make a big difference. However, I also emphasize that you don't have to do everything yourself. Decide early on where you want to invest your time and energy and where it makes more sense to outsource.

5. Failing to Think Long-Term
Publishing isn't a one-and-done process. If you plan to publish multiple books, each one is a learning opportunity. With every book you create, you'll refine your skills, expand your knowledge, and improve your processes. Think of your books as intellectual property that you can build upon, not just a single project to check off your list.

In addition, it's important to understand some basic publishing terms:

1. **ISBN (International Standard Book Number):** A unique identifier for books, essential for retail and library distribution.

2. **Metadata:** Information about your book, including title, author, description, keywords, and categories, used to optimize discoverabil-

ity.

3. **Trim Size:** The dimensions of your printed book.

4. **Royalties:** The percentage of sales revenue an author earns from their book.

5. **Advance:** A payment made to an author before their book earns royalties.

6. **Preassigned Control Number (PCN):** A Library of Congress number assigned before a book is published.

7. **Proof Copy:** A printed version of your book for review before final publication.

8. **ARC (Advanced Reader Copy):** The PDF copy you will give your review teams and early readers

Reflections

1. Have you identified specific areas in your manuscript that need improvement? What steps can you take to address them?

2. What tools or resources do you plan to use for self-editing or hiring professional help?

3. How will you ensure that your book's formatting aligns with industry standards and enhances readability?

Checklist

1. Complete the first draft of your manuscript.

2. Hire a professional editor for developmental editing.

3. Conduct self-editing rounds for grammar and structure.

4. Utilize tools like Grammarly or ProWritingAid for final proofreading.

5. Format your manuscript for print and eBook formats using Atticus or Vellum.

6. Review formatting proofs to ensure consistency.

7. Create a professional book cover, either DIY with Canva or by hiring a designer on Fiverr or 99designs.

"DO NOT GO WHERE THE PATH MAY LEAD, GO INSTEAD WHERE THERE IS NO PATH AND LEAVE A TRAIL."

Ralph Waldo Emerson

Chapter 2

Using AI as an Assistant not a Replacement

Listen, I get it. There is a lot of controversy surrounding AI and creative pursuits, especially when it comes to writing your book. But let me reassure you: AI can be an incredible tool to assist in the creative process, rather than something that takes over altogether. That being said, while it is technically possible to write an entire book in a day using AI, the truth is that you still have to put in the work—organizing the content, enriching the details, and ensuring the information is accurate. If you're a writer who wants to bring your unique ideas into the world, AI is here to enhance your creativity, not replace it.

Making AI Your Writing Assistant

Using AI in your writing can be both fun and simple. For example, in my upcoming book, *Writing with the Archetypes*, which I plan to publish in 2025, I leaned on AI to help flesh out certain aspects. After conceptualizing the idea and identifying the archetypes based on mythology, modern and classical psychology, I used AI to deepen my understanding. For instance, I wasn't sure which zodiac signs aligned with specific archetypes. By feeding AI the relevant archetypes, I asked it to suggest zodiac signs and Myers-Briggs typologies. While AI's suggestions were helpful, I double-checked everything and made adjustments where needed to ensure accuracy.

Another way I used AI was during the editing process. I started with a short manuscript, maybe 500 or 600 words, and asked AI to perform light copyediting while keeping my voice intact. This approach allowed me to clean up my writing without losing its essence. Here's a tip: Copy and paste your text into ChatGPT or another AI platform and ask for light editing. Then, review the changes to ensure everything aligns with your vision. It's efficient, effective, and keeps the final product truly yours.

Leveraging AI for Efficiency

One method I find incredibly useful is dictating my thoughts into my phone and converting the recording into text using tools like SpeechNotes. From there, I input the text into AI for a quick polish. This method is conversational and allows me to capture ideas as they come, while AI helps refine the output.

AI can also assist with other tasks like designing mock-ups for your book cover. While I don't recommend using AI-generated images as your final design, these mock-ups can inspire you or your designer to create something truly unique. Request several options, then cherry-pick the elements you like best.

Deep Insights from AI

If you have access to an upgraded version of AI, such as ChatGPT Pro, you can attach your entire manuscript and ask for insights. Here are some questions you might ask:

- What are the top 15 benefits of this manuscript?
- What demographic would benefit the most from this book?
- What's the estimated reading level of this manuscript?

These insights can be invaluable for marketing and fine-tuning your content. For most books, aim for a reading level between 8th and 10th grade to ensure clarity and accessibility. Simplicity doesn't detract from your work; instead, it makes it more approachable and impactful for a broader audience.

AI for Marketing and Promotion

Marketing can be daunting, especially for introverted creators. AI can help bridge that gap by crafting compelling social media posts, creating content calendars, and even developing a book launch plan. Use it to generate posts that highlight your book's value, create excitement, and engage with potential readers. AI can act as a supportive friend, helping you amplify your work in ways you might hesitate to do yourself.

The Role of AI in Building Confidence

AI has not only helped me become a more efficient writer but also boosted my confidence. By observing how AI refines my work, I've learned to write more clearly and effectively. This process has improved my skills and deepened my appreciation for the art of writing. Remember, AI is a tool to support your creativity, not a substitute for it.

Endless Possibilities

The possibilities with AI are endless. Whether you're using it to generate ideas, perform research, or refine your writing, it's a resource worth exploring. Platforms like ChatGPT and Claude offer powerful features for writers. For just $20 a month, you can unlock tools that enhance your writing process, help you understand trends, and even provide inspiration for future projects.

I am going to be diving into Claude which is primarily used for writing in the future and will give updates on my website via my blog www.asyouwishpublishing.com/blog.

> Did you notice what I did there? I used this part of the book to send you back to my website. Be sure to do this with your books also. Help them continue to conversation beyond your book and they may be interested in purchasing your other books, products or services.

Follow me to the next chapter where we will discuss the types of books you can publish with the information you will learn in this book!

> "EVERY GREAT CHANGE IS PRECEDED BY CHAOS."

Deepak Chopra

Chapter 3
Types of Books Authors Can Publish

In this chapter, we'll explore the various types of books you can create and how to publish them effectively. Whether you're a budding author or an experienced writer, understanding the nuances of different book types can help you make informed decisions. Each type of book has its own unique considerations, from formatting to design, and the right tools can make the process much smoother.

To get started, you'll need the proper tools. Some are essential for any publishing endeavor, while others are optional but can significantly enhance your chances of success. Let's dive into the types of books you can publish and how to bring them to life.

Essential Tools for Publishing

Every author needs the right tools to streamline their publishing process. Tools like **Atticus.io** help with formatting and organization, while **Canva** is excellent for designing stunning book covers and images. If you're aiming to rank your book on platforms like Amazon, consider using **Publisher Rocket** for keyword research and category selection, or **KDSpy** for competitor analysis.

If you're keeping it simple, Atticus and Canva will suffice for most projects. However, those looking to achieve bestseller status or gain broader visibility should explore the additional tools available. With these essentials in hand, you're ready to explore specific book types.

Another essential tool is Adobe Acrobat DC. You are able to edit your PDF and make sure that the details are exactly they way you want them to look. Atticus is amazing at getting the bones of your manuscript professionally designed, but Adobe Acrobat fine tunes the manuscript and helps you to fix any erros quickly. You can also delete or add pages, change some of the fonts. We typically see this on the title page. But do recommend that you use a replica of your book cover title page if you can. But if you want to make a major overall changes going back to Atticus and making the changes there will be much more efficient.

Fiction and Nonfiction Books

Fiction and nonfiction books are among the most popular and versatile genres for authors. Fiction is all about storytelling, where a continuous narrative captivates the reader from beginning to end. Nonfiction, on the other hand, often provides value through actionable insights, advice, or educational content. Both genres require attention to formatting and design, but their structures differ significantly.

When writing fiction, your primary focus is on the narrative. Fiction books typically have straightforward chapter divisions and may include decorative elements for scene breaks. Nonfiction books, however, often include features like bullet points, thoughtful questions, or action steps to engage the reader and encourage interaction. These distinctions make nonfiction an excellent tool for coaches, business owners, or mentors aiming to guide readers to a larger offering or service.

Key Tool: Atticus.io
Atticus simplifies the formatting process for both fiction and nonfiction, ensuring your book is professional and polished. You can also use it to easily incorporate

additional features, like illustrations or structured elements, based on your book's needs.

Collaborative Anthologies

Collaborative anthologies are a fantastic way to bring together multiple voices under one theme. These books are often created around a specific topic, such as self-help, spirituality, or business, and feature contributions from various authors. They are not only a wonderful community-building project but also a profitable endeavor when managed effectively.

To create a successful anthology, start by selecting a compelling theme. You can attract contributors by sharing a draft cover design and outlining the benefits of participating. Pricing can vary widely, from $200 to $500 or more per author, depending on the added perks like marketing, interviews, or exclusive classes. Including author bios, images, or QR codes can enhance the book's appeal and provide additional exposure for contributors.

Specialty of As You Wish Publishing

At As You Wish Publishing, we've perfected the art of creating anthologies that build connections and generate income. From hosting launch parties to including exclusive content, anthologies are a powerful tool for collaboration and creativity.

Children's Books

Children's books are vibrant, colorful, and full of wonder. They require a keen eye for design and an understanding of what captures a child's imagination. From selecting the right illustrator to ensuring the durability of the final product, creating a children's book can be both rewarding and challenging.

Illustrations play a central role in children's books, and hiring a skilled illustrator is crucial. Platforms like Fiverr or Upwork are excellent places to find talented artists, but costs can range from $600 to $3,000 depending on the project's scope. For those on a budget, Canva or AI-generated images are viable options, but ensure your designs meet the required specifications for trim size and bleed settings.

You can create your designs in Canva even the free version will work just fine. Keep in mind you must make sure that your design goes beyond the bleed size for images. For example you will want to size a 8.5 x 8.5 book to 8.625 x 8.75 and the image must go to the bleed edge. If there is any lettering in that bleed area it will be cut off. Use this guide on KDP to determine what size you will need your book pages to be: https://kdp.amazon.com/en_US/help/topic/GVBQ3CMEQW3W2VL6

Durability and Design

Since children's books are often handled roughly, use premium pages and glossy covers to enhance their durability. You can also explore crowdfunding or pre-orders to finance illustrations and production.

Journals and Low-Content Books

Journals, planners, and low-content books are ideal for authors looking for a simpler publishing process. These books often feature minimal text and rely heavily on their cover designs to attract buyers. Despite their simplicity, they serve a wide audience, from individuals seeking daily affirmations to those who want guided prompts.

Creating a journal is straightforward with tools like Tangent Templates. You can choose from a variety of page layouts, such as lined pages, prompts, or calendar templates. This flexibility allows you to cater to specific niches, such as gratitude journals, planners, or affirmation books, with minimal effort.

Key Tool: Tangent Templates
With Tangent Templates, you can easily create professional interiors for low-content books. Pair these with a striking cover, and you're ready to publish.

Picture Books

Picture books are perfect for visual storytelling and make great coffee table or keepsake books. They require high-quality images and careful design to create an engaging reader experience. Whether for children or adults, picture books are a versatile option for authors who want to combine visual and textual elements.

Using Canva, you can design layouts that incorporate images and text seamlessly. For hardcover editions, platforms like Lulu.com or KDP provide excellent options. Remember to use premium materials for vibrant, glossy pages, and ensure your trim size and bleed settings are accurate.

Flexible Options
Picture books can be published as hardcovers or paperbacks, with high-quality color pages that elevate the book's overall appeal. While color pages can be costly, they add a professional touch to your work.

Puzzle Books

Puzzle books are a fun and engaging way to reach a wide audience. From word searches to Sudoku and mazes, these books provide interactive entertainment for readers of all ages. They're especially popular as gifts or supplemental activities for children's books.

Book Bolt is the go-to tool for creating puzzle books. It offers templates for various puzzles, making it easy to design and customize your content. You can even use puzzles as a supplementary feature in other book types, such as adding a maze or crossword puzzle to a children's book.

Key Tool: Book Bolt
With Book Bolt, you can create dynamic and interactive puzzle books, expanding your catalog with ease.

Poetry and Meditation Books

Poetry and meditation books offer authors the chance to express creativity and provide readers with inspiration and calm. These books can be standalone projects or collaborative anthologies, depending on your vision. Adding visuals or formatting meditations with thoughtful spacing enhances the reader's experience.

You can pair poems or meditations with images to create a visually rich book. Collaborating with other poets or writers can also add diversity and depth to the content. Whether you focus on themed anthologies or standalone works, the possibilities are endless.

Versatility
Poetry and meditation books are perfect for print and digital formats, allowing you to reach a broader audience with creative and impactful content.

Final Thoughts on Publishing

The key to success is proper formatting and an eye-catching book cover. With the right tools and some creativity, there's no limit to the types of books you can publish. Whether you're creating a novel, journal, or anthology, the possibilities are endless!

> "WRITE THE BOOK YOU WANT TO READ."
>
> *Toni Morrison*

Chapter 4

Understanding Publishing Platforms

Publishing platforms are the gateway to getting your book into the hands of readers around the world. Each platform offers unique features and advantages, so it's important to choose the ones that align with your goals. In this chapter, we'll introduce the major platforms and provide insights to help you make informed decisions.

Overview of Major Platforms

- **Kindle Direct Publishing (KDP):** As Amazon's self-publishing platform, KDP is one of the most popular and accessible options for independent authors. It allows you to publish eBooks, paperbacks, and even hardcover books, all with global distribution. KDP's user-friendly interface and direct integration with Amazon's marketplace make it a top choice for many authors. Additionally, KDP offers competitive royalty rates and promotional tools, such as Kindle Countdown Deals and free promotions, to boost your book's visibility.

- **IngramSpark:** Known for its extensive distribution network, IngramSpark is ideal for authors who want to reach bookstores, libraries, and online retailers. Unlike KDP, which focuses on Amazon's ecosystem, IngramSpark provides access to a broader market. This platform is particularly valuable for authors aiming for wide distribution and a professional presence in the industry. However, it requires upfront fees and offers less intuitive tools compared to KDP.

- **Draft2Digital:** Draft2Digital simplifies the publishing process by acting as an aggregator, distributing your eBook to multiple platforms, including Apple Books, Barnes & Noble, and Kobo. It's a great choice for authors who prefer a hands-off approach to managing multiple accounts. Draft2Digital also provides a free formatting tool, making it easy to prepare your manuscript for publication.

Comparison of Features, Royalties, and Distribution Options

Each platform has its strengths, and understanding these can help you choose the best fit for your goals. KDP excels in Amazon-centric distribution and marketing, while IngramSpark shines in providing a professional edge and access to brick-and-mortar bookstores. Draft2Digital, on the other hand, offers simplicity and reach without the need for upfront fees. Consider factors such as royalties, ease of use, and distribution reach when deciding which platform(s) to use.

Deciding Which Platform(s) to Use

Selecting the right platform depends on your publishing objectives. Are you focused on maximizing sales through Amazon? KDP might be your best bet. Do you want your book available in libraries and independent bookstores? IngramSpark can help. For authors who prioritize convenience and wide digital distribution, Draft2Digital offers an excellent solution. You can also use a combination of platforms to leverage the strengths of each. For instance, many authors publish paperbacks through IngramSpark and eBooks through KDP to optimize their reach.

By understanding the options available and aligning them with your goals, you can create a publishing strategy that works for you. In the next chapter, we'll delve into the step-by-step process of publishing with KDP, giving you a detailed walkthrough of this popular platform.

Primary Issues with Platforms

When it comes to publishing platforms, the main ones we'll be focusing on are Kindle Direct Publishing (KDP), IngramSpark, Draft2Digital, and Audible. Each platform has its own set of rules and requirements, and if you don't follow them correctly, your book might get rejected.

Based on my nearly nine years of experience, the most common issues arise from formatting problems, errors in the manuscript, or book cover design issues—especially when the cover doesn't extend properly to the bleed area. These are the primary pitfalls I've encountered over the years.

Another issue I ran into involved ISBNs. I had a book on KDP with expanded distribution enabled, which prevented me from using the same ISBN to publish the book on IngramSpark. The solution was to purchase a new ISBN and use that for IngramSpark. While there are workarounds for some challenges, not all issues can be resolved so easily.

Here are a few other pitfalls to keep in mind:

- **KDP Select and Draft2Digital**: If your book is enrolled in KDP Select (which includes Kindle Unlimited), you can't publish it on Draft2Digital until it's out of the KDP Select exclusivity period. Additionally, if you use KDP's AI-generated audio feature, your book must remain in KDP Select—it can't be published elsewhere.

- **Platform Nuances**: Each platform has its quirks, and it's essential to read the fine print. For example, Draft2Digital and KDP Select have specific rules about promotions and exclusivity, and ignoring them could result in your book being removed from one platform or another.

Despite these challenges, I recommend publishing your book on as many platforms as possible to maximize residual income. I personally feel the most comfortable with KDP. It is the first platform I learned on and I feel the most at ease with it's functionality. I appreciate the customer service and I've made every mistake imaginable while using it. That being said I've heard that other authors felt more comfortable and liked the quality of IngramSpark.

The key is to familiarize yourself with each platform's requirements and be strategic about how and when you publish. Diversifying across multiple platforms ensures your book reaches a wider audience and creates multiple streams of revenue.

Reflections

1. Which publishing platform(s) align best with your publishing goals and target audience?

2. Are there features or benefits of specific platforms that you find most appealing? Why?

3. What concerns or challenges do you anticipate when navigating these platforms, and how can you prepare for them?

Checklist

1. Research publishing platforms: KDP, IngramSpark, Draft2Digital.

2. Compare platform royalties and distribution options.

3. Decide on exclusive vs. wide distribution strategies.

4. Sign up and create accounts on your chosen

platforms.

5. Familiarize yourself with the platform interfaces and features.

"TO BE YOURSELF IN A WORLD THAT IS CONSTANTLY TRYING TO MAKE YOU SOMETHING ELSE IS THE GREATEST ACCOMPLISHMENT."

Ralph Waldo Emerson

Chapter 5

Step-by-Step Guide to Publishing with KDP

Publishing with Kindle Direct Publishing (KDP) is a streamlined process that allows authors to self-publish their work and reach a global audience through Amazon's vast marketplace. In this chapter, we will break down each step to help you navigate KDP with confidence and ensure your book is published professionally.

Creating an Account on KDP

To begin, you'll need an Amazon account. If you already shop on Amazon, you can use the same credentials to log in to KDP. Visit the KDP website and sign in to set up your publishing account. Once logged in, provide essential details such as your tax information and bank account for royalty payments. This initial setup ensures you're ready to start uploading your book files.

Creating an account is straightforward, but accuracy is crucial when entering personal and financial information. Double-check your tax details to avoid delays in receiving payments. KDP's interface is user-friendly, guiding you through each step to complete your profile.

How to Create a KDP Account

Already Have an Amazon Account?

If you already have an Amazon account, you can use it to sign in to Kindle Direct Publishing (KDP). Here's how:

1. Go to https://kdp.amazon.com.

2. Under "Sign in with your Amazon account," click **Sign in**.

3. Enter your email address and password, then click **Sign in**.

4. Once logged in, you'll be directed to your KDP Bookshelf.

Don't Have an Amazon Account?

Follow these steps to create a KDP account:

1. Go to https://kdp.amazon.com/ and click **Sign up**.

2. Click **Create your KDP account**.

3. Enter your name, email address, and a secure password.

4. After creating your account, you'll need to provide author, payment, and tax information. Follow the steps below to complete the setup. The author name (your legal name) and pen name can be different for your books.

Setting Up Your Account Profile

Author/Publisher Information

1. Select a **Business type** (individual or corporation).

2. Enter your first and last name, or the name of your publishing company. Avoid using pen names or special characters (e.g., & ! ? #).

3. Provide a valid mailing address for tax reporting purposes and royalty payments. If prompted, confirm the suggested address.

4. Click **Save**.

Note: The name you provide must be your legal name. Payments and tax forms will be issued under this name. You can use a pen name when setting up book details; refer to the "Authors & Contributors" section for instructions on managing pen names.

Getting Paid

KDP offers various payment methods, including direct deposit, wire transfer, and check. Amazon Payments and PayPal are not supported.

To Add a Bank Account:

1. Log in to your KDP account.

2. Complete two-step verification.

3. Under **Getting Paid**, click **Add a bank account**.

4. Enter your bank account details according to your country/region requirements.

5. Select **Add my bank account**, then click **Add**.

6. A green checkmark will confirm successful set-up.

7. Click **Save**.

Note: If your bank's location isn't listed, KDP may not support direct deposit or wire transfer for that region. Visit https://kdp.amazon.com/ for alternative methods.

Important: Ensure the account holder's name matches the bank account records exactly. Mismatches may prevent deposits.

Providing Tax Information

Amazon requires all publishers to provide valid taxpayer identification to comply with U.S. tax regulations. Requirements vary depending on whether you are a U.S. or non-U.S. citizen.

To Complete Your Tax Information:

1. Go to **Your Account**.

2. Select **Tax Information**.

3. Click **Complete Tax Questionnaire** (or **Update/Access Tax Profile** if updating).

4. Enter your Tax Profile information and click **Complete Tax Questionnaire** to save your changes.

Non-U.S. Publishers: If you're claiming tax treaty benefits to reduce withholding, provide a valid Tax Identification Number (TIN).

For more details, visit. https://kdp.amazon.com/

Uploading Your Manuscript and Cover

Once your account is set up, navigate to the "Bookshelf" tab and select "Create a New Title." Here, you'll provide basic details about your book, including its title, subtitle, and description. These elements play a critical role in attracting potential readers, so ensure they are clear, concise, and compelling.

When uploading your manuscript, ensure it is properly formatted for print or digital publication. KDP accepts various file types, including DOCX and PDF for print and MOBI for Kindle eBooks. For your cover, you can upload a pre-designed file or use KDP's Cover Creator to design one on the platform. Ensure your cover file meets KDP's size and resolution requirements to avoid submission issues.

Setting Up Your Book Details

After uploading your files, you'll need to provide additional details, including:

- **Keywords:** Select up to seven keywords or

phrases that potential readers might use to find your book.

- **Categories:** Choose two categories that best match your book's genre and content. Tools like Publisher Rocket can help identify optimal categories to increase visibility.

- **ISBN:** If you're publishing a print book, you can use a free ISBN from KDP or purchase your own through Bowker to maintain full control over your publishing rights.

Completing this step ensures your book appears in the right searches and categories, maximizing its discoverability on Amazon's platform.

Choosing Pricing and Royalties

KDP offers two royalty options: 35% and 70%. The higher royalty tier is available for eBooks priced between $2.99 and $9.99, while the 35% option applies to other price ranges. Set a competitive price based on your book's genre, length, and comparable titles in the market. Remember to account for printing costs when pricing paperback editions.

By following these steps, you'll have your book ready for publication on KDP. In the next chapter, we'll explore how to use IngramSpark for broader distribution and professional publishing options.

Pitfalls with KDP

KDP (Kindle Direct Publishing) tends to keep books within its own ecosystem and places restrictions on where else you can publish. For example, if your eBook is enrolled in KDP Select (which includes Kindle Unlimited), you cannot publish that book on Draft2Digital, even if you change or add an ISBN number.

One major thing to watch for is understanding what each KDP feature restricts you from doing. For instance, if you enroll in KDP Unlimited to run a free book promotion, you won't be able to publish your book on Draft2Digital or other similar platforms during the exclusivity period. There may be additional restrictions depending on the options you choose, so it's crucial to read the fine print. Make sure you're clear about what you're agreeing to before proceeding.

Reflections

1. Have you finalized all metadata (title, subtitle, description, keywords) for your book? How do they reflect your target audience's interests?

2. Are you planning to use a free ISBN from KDP

or purchase your own? Why?

3. What pricing strategy will you adopt for your book, and how does it compare to similar titles in your genre?

Checklist

1. Set up an account on KDP.

2. Upload your manuscript and cover.

3. Enter metadata, including title, keywords, and categories.

4. Assign an ISBN (use a free one from KDP or purchase your own).

5. Set book pricing and select royalty options.

6. Review and approve a proof copy.

7. Publish your book and monitor its performance.

"COURAGE IS TAKING ACTION IN THE PRESENCE OF RISK, IN SPITE OF FEAR."

―― Sean Platt

Chapter 6

Step-by-Step Guide to Publishing with IngramSpark

IngramSpark is a powerful platform for authors who want to expand their distribution network beyond Amazon. With its access to bookstores, libraries, and global markets, IngramSpark offers unparalleled opportunities for wide reach. This chapter provides a detailed walkthrough of how to publish your book using this platform.

Setting Up an Account

The first step in using IngramSpark is creating an account. Visit the IngramSpark website https://myaccount.ingramspark.com/Account/Sign upand sign up as a new user. During registration, you'll need to provide information about yourself and your publishing entity. If you plan to establish your own publishing imprint, ensure you have all necessary details ready, such as a business name and tax identification number.

IngramSpark requires an upfront setup fee for each title you publish. While this might seem like a drawback compared to KDP's free setup, the investment grants access to an extensive distribution network. Consider this fee as part of your professional publishing strategy, particularly if your goal is to see your book in bookstores and libraries.

Be sure to have the following information before attempting to set up your account:

- Valid email address

- Credit card to keep on file in your secure account (can be changed at any time or others added)

- Tax ID numbers can be provided for business accounts

- Banking information or PayPal information (US) (for direct deposit of what you earn for every book sale)

Understanding ISBN Requirements

An International Standard Book Number (ISBN) is essential for publishing with IngramSpark. Unlike KDP, IngramSpark does not provide free ISBNs, meaning you'll need to purchase one from Bowker or your country's equivalent ISBN agency. Owning your ISBN ensures you retain full control over your publishing rights.

When purchasing an ISBN, you can assign it to your print and digital editions. Keep in mind that each format (e.g., paperback, hardcover, eBook) requires a unique ISBN. Maintaining a record of your assigned ISBNs will help you manage your catalog effectively as your publishing business grows.

Uploading Files and Selecting Print Options

With your account set up and ISBN ready, you can begin uploading your manuscript and cover files. IngramSpark provides detailed file specifications to ensure compatibility with their printing systems. Pay close attention to their requirements for margins, bleed, and file resolution to avoid delays during the review process.

IngramSpark offers a variety of print options, including hardcover, paperback, and different trim sizes. These options allow you to tailor your book to meet the expectations of your target audience. Additionally, you can choose from various paper types and binding styles to create a professional and visually appealing product.

For the complete set up guide provided by Ingram Spark visit this link: https://tinyurl.com/yz6pn792 or use this QR Code

Setting Wholesale Discounts and Returns Policies

One of IngramSpark's unique features is its flexibility in setting wholesale discounts and returns policies. These options are critical for authors targeting the traditional retail market. Wholesale discounts typically range from 30% to 55%, and offering a competitive discount can make your book more attractive to retailers.

Returns policies are another important consideration. While allowing returns increases your book's appeal to bookstores, it also introduces the risk of returned stock costs. Evaluate your financial situation and market goals before deciding on your returns policy.

Pitfalls with IngramSpark

IngramSpark can be very finicky, and dealing with their customer service can be a frustrating experience. To avoid delays, it's best to get everything right the first time. I highly recommend watching tutorials on YouTube about how to upload your book to IngramSpark properly.

Here are a few key points to keep in mind:

1. **Barcodes**: You can either have IngramSpark generate a barcode for you or purchase one separately from a provider like Bowker for about $25. Personally, I prefer using the barcode from the proof IngramSpark provides.

2. **Rejections**: If your book is rejected, it can take a long time to fix the issue and have it approved. This is another reason to ensure you understand the process fully before uploading your book.

3. **Book Format**: I only use IngramSpark for print versions because that's what independent bookstores require. Their print costs aren't great—more expensive than KDP—and I don't think the quality is as good as KDP. However, independent bookstores favor IngramSpark because it allows them to return unsold books and

get their money back.

Returns and Costs for Authors
For authors, the return policy means that bookstores can return unsold books, which comes out of your royalties. Additionally, you have two choices for those returned books:

1. **Destroy the Books**: This means you won't have to deal with them, but they're gone for good.

2. **Ship the Books to Yourself**: This option incurs a shipping cost, and the condition of the books may not be ideal (e.g., they might be damaged or unsellable).

This return policy can lead to added costs and challenges, especially if you're not planning to host book signings or other events where you could use returned books.

Is It Worth It?
IngramSpark is essential if you want to get your book into independent bookstores or go on a book tour. However, it's a tradeoff: while it offers access to bookstores, the potential costs and challenges of returns can add up. It's really a matter of weighing the benefits against the hardships. For me, it's a "six of one, half a dozen of the other" situation. The value of

IngramSpark depends entirely on what you want to achieve with your book.

Reflections

1. How will you leverage IngramSparks advantage of reaching bookstores and libraries?

2. Have you decided on your wholesale discount and returns policy? What factors influenced your decision?

3. How will you ensure that your print files meet IngramSpark's technical specifications to avoid delays?

Checklist

1. Register an account with IngramSpark.

2. Purchase ISBNs from Bowker (if not already obtained).

3. Prepare and upload print-ready files.

4. Set wholesale discounts and returns policy.

5. Review and approve the proof copy.

6. Distribute to bookstores, libraries, and online retailers.

> "WRITING IS THE ACT OF DISCOVERING WHAT YOU BELIEVE."
>
> *David Hare*

Chapter 7

Step-by-Step Guide to Publishing with Draft2Digital

Draft2Digital (D2D) is a user-friendly platform that simplifies the process of distributing your eBook to multiple digital retailers. With its intuitive interface and valuable features, it's an excellent choice for authors looking for hassle-free eBook publishing. This chapter provides a comprehensive guide to publishing with Draft2Digital.

Overview of the Platform's Unique Benefits

Draft2Digital sets itself apart from other platforms by offering a streamlined approach to eBook publishing. Its free formatting tool allows you to create a professional eBook without requiring advanced technical skills. Additionally, D2D provides wide distribution to major retailers, including Apple Books, Barnes & Noble, Kobo, and more. Unlike other platforms, there are no upfront costs—Draft2Digital takes a percentage of your royalties as payment, making it a low-risk option for authors.

Another significant benefit is the ability to manage all your eBook distribution in one place. With a single upload, you can reach multiple platforms, saving you time and effort. D2D also offers robust author support and analytics to help you monitor your book's performance across different retailers.

Setting Up an Account

To get started with Draft2Digital, visit their website and sign up for a free account. The registration process is straightforward, requiring basic information such as your name, email, and payment details. Once your account is created, you'll have access to the author dashboard, where you can manage your books and track royalties.

Setting up your account includes linking your bank or PayPal account for royalty payments. Draft2Digital pays royalties monthly, making it easier to keep track of your earnings. Providing accurate payment and tax information during the setup process ensures there are no delays in receiving your funds.

Uploading Your Manuscript and Metadata

Draft2Digital's uploading process is simple and efficient. Start by uploading your manuscript file in a compatible format, such as DOCX or RTF. D2D's formatting tool automatically converts your file into a professionally styled eBook. You can preview and make adjustments to the layout before finalizing your submission.

Next, enter your book's metadata, including title, author name, description, and keywords. Metadata plays a crucial role in helping potential readers discover your book, so take the time to craft a compelling and accurate description. You'll also select genres and categories that best match your book's content.

Choosing Distribution Partners

One of Draft2Digital's strengths is its extensive network of distribution partners. After uploading your manuscript, you'll have the option to select which retailers and platforms you want to distribute your book to. Popular options include Apple Books, Barnes & Noble, Kobo, Tolino, and Scribd. You can also opt into Draft2Digital's library distribution service to reach readers in schools and libraries. I have heard of one issue with Hoopla. It seems that if you want to take your book off of Hoopla it can take longer than usual. I would recommend until that is resolved you opt not to choose them on D2D's list of distribution partners.

If you prefer to manage your Amazon distribution separately, you can exclude Kindle from your distribution list. This flexibility allows you to tailor your strategy to meet your goals. Please keep in mind that you will not be able to publish your ebook with Draft2Digital if your ebook is subscribed to Kindle Unlimited (KU). I can be up on KDP but if you opt to have it on KU for marketing purposes (free promotions etc.) Draft2Digital will reject the book. Even if you try to use a different ISBN it still won't upload. Also, if you use the free Virtual Voice AI for Kindle, you must be enrolled in KU. You wont be able to add your Kindle Virtual Voice ebooks to Draft2Digital.

Managing Payments and Reporting

Draft2Digital provides transparent reporting tools to track your book's performance. The author dashboard displays sales data across all distribution channels, giving you valuable insights into where your book is performing best. Monthly royalty payments are deposited directly into your linked account, making it easy to manage your earnings.

By following these steps, you can successfully publish your eBook with Draft2Digital and take advantage of its wide-reaching distribution network. In the next chapter, we'll explore the process of creating audiobooks with Audible's ACX platform.

Reflections

1. Which distribution partners will you prioritize through Draft2Digital, and why?

2. How do you plan to use Draft2Digital's free formatting tools to create a professional eBook?

3. What steps will you take to ensure consistency across multiple distribution channels?

Checklist

1. Create a free Draft2Digital account.

2. Upload your manuscript and customize eBook formatting.

3. Enter metadata and select distribution partners.

4. Review the generated eBook preview.

5. Publish and manage your sales dashboard.

"THE STORIES WE TELL OURSELVES AND SHARE WITH THE WORLD HAVE THE POWER TO SHAPE THE LIVES OF OTHERS."

Brené Brown

Chapter 8

Creating Audiobooks with Audible (ACX)

Audiobooks have become an essential format for authors seeking to expand their reach and cater to a growing audience of audio listeners. Audible's ACX platform is one of the most popular tools for creating and distributing audiobooks. This chapter will guide you through the process of bringing your book to life in audio format.

Why Audiobooks Matter

Audiobooks offer a unique way to connect with readers who prefer listening over reading. With the rise of smartphones and audio streaming services, the demand for audiobooks has skyrocketed. Adding an audiobook version of your book can significantly increase your audience reach and generate additional revenue streams. Furthermore, audiobooks provide an opportunity to bring a new dimension to your story, with professional narration enhancing the experience for listeners.

Creating an audiobook may seem daunting at first, but platforms like ACX simplify the process by providing the tools and resources you need. Whether you choose to narrate the book yourself or hire a professional narrator, ACX offers a clear path to publication and distribution.

Setting Up an ACX Account

To get started, visit the ACX website: https://www.acx.com/ and sign up for an account. If you already have an Amazon account, you can use it to log in. Once logged in, you'll need to provide some basic information about yourself and your book.

ACX allows authors to choose how they want to produce their audiobook: through a royalty-share agreement with a narrator, by paying a flat fee to a narrator, or by recording the book themselves. During the setup process, you'll also need to link your audiobook to the eBook or print version available on Amazon to establish credibility and ensure proper metadata.

Choosing Between Hiring a Narrator or DIY Recording

- **Hiring a Professional Narrator:** Hiring a narrator ensures a polished and engaging audiobook. ACX connects authors with a vast network of professional voice actors. You can browse narrators based on their style, voice tone, and experience, and even listen to samples before making a decision. Royalty-share agreements are a cost-effective way to work with talented narrators, as they receive a percentage of your audiobook's sales instead of an upfront fee.

- **DIY Recording:** If you have a clear and engaging voice, recording your audiobook yourself can be a rewarding option. This approach is ideal for memoirs, self-help books, or works where a personal touch enhances the connection with listeners. To record your audiobook, you'll need a quiet recording space, quality microphone, and audio editing software such as Audacity or GarageBand. ACX provides detailed guidelines to ensure your recordings meet their technical requirements.

Uploading and Finalizing Audiobook Files

Once your audiobook has been recorded, the next step is to upload the audio files to ACX. Ensure that your files meet ACX's technical specifications, including:

- Audio recorded in mono or stereo, at a sample rate of 44.1 kHz.

- Each chapter as a separate audio file, with consistent opening and closing credits.

- Files exported in MP3 format with a constant bit rate of 192 kbps.

ACX provides a quality check service to review your files for compliance. After approval, your audiobook will be distributed through Audible, Amazon, and iTunes, reaching millions of potential listeners.

New Offer from KDP, AI Generated Audio Books

KDP now offers a way to generate audiobooks using AI directly within your KDP account. This is something many people struggle with, and that's understandable. However, it's a great option if you can't afford to hire a narrator or don't have the equipment to produce high-quality audio yourself.

To use this feature, there are a few things you need to know. First, your book must have an eBook version, and it must be enrolled in Kindle Unlimited. Without that, the option won't be available.

The process is simple and doesn't take much time to set up. Once your book is published, you may see an option to "Add audiobook with virtual voice." If you're interested, click the button and follow the straightforward, step-by-step instructions. You can choose the voice style and even ensure specific words are pronounced correctly.

You'll also have control over pricing and can choose to link the audiobook to your eBook for a discount if you'd like. This feature is efficient and can help you get your audiobook published quickly. Keep in mind, your sales and reporting will be managed through your KDP account, not ACX.

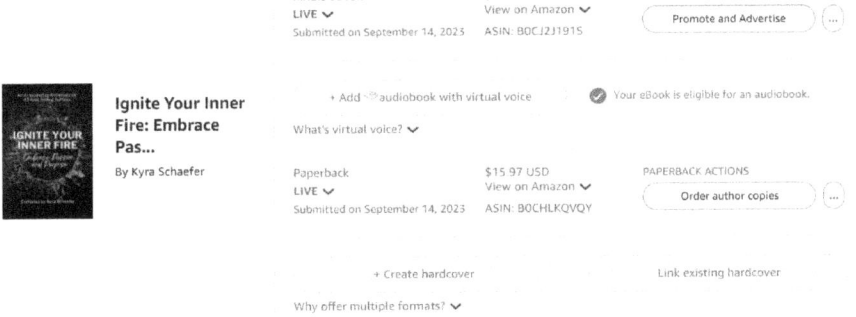

Distribution and Royalties

ACX offers several royalty options based on the distribution exclusivity you choose. Opting for exclusive distribution provides higher royalty rates (up to 40%), while non-exclusive distribution allows you to sell your audiobook on other platforms but at a lower royalty rate (25%).

Understanding your target audience and distribution goals will help you decide which option best aligns with your publishing strategy. Once your audiobook is live, monitor its performance using ACX's reporting tools and promote it alongside your eBook or print version to maximize sales.

By following these steps, you can successfully create and distribute an audiobook that expands your book's reach and enhances its impact. In the next chapter, we'll delve into the process of setting up a publisher imprint to establish your publishing identity.

Reflections

1. Will you narrate your audiobook or hire a professional narrator? What influenced your decision?

2. How will you ensure that your audio files meet ACX's quality standards?

3. Which distribution model (exclusive or non-exclusive) will you choose for your audiobook, and why?

Checklist

1. Sign up for an ACX account.

2. Decide between self-narration or hiring a professional.

3. Record and edit audiobook files to meet ACX standards.

4. Upload and review audio files for quality.

5. Select distribution options (exclusive or non-exclusive).

6. Approve for publication on Audible, Amazon, and iTunes.

"YOU OWE IT TO YOURSELF TO BELIEVE IN THE VOICE THAT KEEPS WHISPERING, 'THIS IS WORTH SHARING.'"

Unknown

Chapter 9

Setting Up A Publisher Imprint

Establishing a publisher imprint is a crucial step for authors who want to take full control of their publishing endeavors. A publisher imprint not only adds professionalism to your books but also helps you build a recognizable brand in the literary world. This chapter will guide you through the process of setting up an imprint, from understanding its importance to obtaining the necessary identifiers and registrations.

What is a Publisher Imprint and Why it Matters

A publisher imprint is the trade name under which you publish your books. Think of it as your publishing "brand." When readers or retailers see your imprint's name on a book, it signals professionalism and establishes trust. A well-chosen imprint name can also help position your books in the market by aligning with specific genres or audiences.

For self-publishing authors, having a publisher imprint offers additional benefits. It separates your role as an author from your role as a publisher, providing greater credibility. Additionally, it allows you to manage your books under a unified brand, making it easier to scale your publishing business in the future.

Obtaining ISBNs from Bowker

One of the first steps in setting up your imprint is obtaining ISBNs (International Standard Book Numbers). In the United States, Bowker is the official provider of ISBNs. Each ISBN serves as a unique identifier for a specific edition and format of your book, ensuring it is properly cataloged and discoverable by retailers and libraries.

To purchase ISBNs:

1. Visit the Bowker website and create an account.

2. Choose the package that suits your needs—a single ISBN for one book or a block of ISBNs if you plan to publish multiple titles.

3. Once purchased, you can assign ISBNs to your

books through Bowker's MyIdentifiers portal.

Having your own ISBNs, rather than using free ones provided by platforms like KDP, allows you to list your imprint as the publisher of record. This gives you greater control over your book's metadata and distribution.

Applying for a Library of Congress Control Number (LCCN)

For U.S.-based authors, obtaining a Library of Congress Control Number (LCCN) is another step to consider. An LCCN is a unique identifier assigned by the Library of Congress, often used by libraries to catalog books.

To apply for an LCCN:

1. Set up a publisher account with the Library of Congress's Preassigned Control Number (PCN) program.

2. Complete the application form, providing details about your book and publisher imprint.

3. Submit the application and wait for approval. Once approved, the Library of Congress will assign an LCCN to your book.

Having an LCCN adds credibility to your book and increases its accessibility to libraries and educational institutions.

Registering Your Imprint as a Business

To formalize your publisher imprint, consider registering it as a business entity, such as an LLC (Limited Liability Company). Doing so offers legal protection and enables you to open a business bank account, separate your personal and business finances, and claim tax deductions for publishing-related expenses.

1. Choose a name for your imprint and check its availability in your state or country.

2. File the necessary paperwork with your local business registration office.

3. Obtain an EIN (Employer Identification Number) from the IRS for tax purposes.

4. Set up a business bank account to manage your publishing income and expenses.

By establishing your imprint as a legal entity, you'll not only protect your assets but also position yourself for long-term success in the publishing industry.

By following these steps, you'll have a fully operational publisher imprint that enhances your professional image and supports your publishing ambitions. In the next chapter, we'll explore how to start your own publishing business to further expand your reach and opportunities.

Downfalls to Getting an Imprint?

Setting up a publisher imprint doesn't really have many pitfalls or downfalls. The most important thing is to make sure you're happy with the name you choose.

For example, we chose "As You Wish Publishing" because the phrase "as you wish" means "I love you," inspired by *The Princess Bride*. That's how our company came to be—we loved someone, cared about them, missed them, and came together to support each other through the pain of loss. When it came time to name the company, I called it As You Wish Publishing without realizing this would become my life and career.

At the time, I had no idea we would end up publishing hundreds of authors, producing bestselling books on Amazon, and achieving so much more. In the beginning, I just wanted to honor a friend I loved, and that was it. But the work kept growing, and so did the company.

If I could go back, I might do one thing differently. While I'm very attached to the name "As You Wish Publishing" and wouldn't change it now, I've since updated how the business operates. Currently, our tax ID is under "TKSchaefer Enterprises," and we do business as As You Wish Publishing. Originally, the tax ID was tied directly to As You Wish Publishing, which felt limiting. I couldn't easily expand into other areas, like coaching clients or other non-publishing projects I was working on. Having the flexibility to do business under multiple ventures has been incredibly helpful.

If I could offer one piece of advice, it would be this: choose a publisher imprint name that you love—something meaningful that resonates with your mission yet remains distinct from your personal name. Be clear about your company's focus; for example, my company is called As You Wish Publishing, but it's truly a publishing services company. If you're not physically binding books, avoid using "Press" in your name, as it traditionally refers to that specific process. Instead, consider "Publishing" or a term that better reflects your services. Finally, think about the bigger picture. Structuring your business with a more general name or as a parent company for your tax ID can create flexibility for growth and future projects.

Ultimately, setting up a publisher imprint is an exciting and creative process. Have fun with it, be intentional, and enjoy building something meaningful.

Reflections

1. Have you chosen an imprint name that reflects your brand and publishing goals?

2. What steps will you take to formalize your imprint as a business entity?

3. How will owning your ISBNs and applying for an LCCN enhance your professional credibility?

Checklist

1. Choose and register a unique imprint name.

2. Purchase ISBNs under your imprint from Bowker.

3. Apply for a Library of Congress Control Number.

4. File for an LLC to formalize your imprint as a business.

5. Set up a business bank account for financial management.

6. Create a logo and branding materials for your imprint.

"THE COURAGE TO CREATE AND SHARE IS THE BRIDGE BETWEEN WHO YOU ARE AND WHO YOU ARE BECOMING."

Dr. Wayne Dyer

Chapter 10

Starting Your Publishing Business

For authors looking to establish themselves as publishers, starting a publishing business can open new doors. Not only does it provide legal and financial benefits, but it also allows you to expand your publishing efforts beyond your own books. This chapter will guide you through the process of setting up a publishing business, including registering your company, understanding tax implications, and building a foundation for growth.

Benefits of Formalizing Your Publishing Efforts

Starting a publishing business offers several advantages. First and foremost, it separates your personal and professional finances, providing liability protection and enabling better financial management. By establishing a business entity, you can open a business bank account, apply for business credit, and access resources designed specifically for small businesses.

Additionally, running a publishing business allows you to claim tax deductions on expenses such as software, office supplies, marketing, and professional services. This can significantly reduce your overall tax burden, freeing up more resources for reinvestment into your publishing endeavors. Finally, formalizing your efforts positions you as a serious professional in the industry, enhancing your credibility with authors, retailers, and collaborators.

How to File for an LLC (Limited Liability Company)

An LLC is one of the most popular structures for small publishing businesses due to its simplicity and flexibility. Here's how to set up an LLC in the United States:

1. **Choose a Business Name:** Ensure your chosen name is unique and adheres to your state's naming guidelines. Consider using your publisher imprint name as your LLC name to maintain brand consistency.

2. **File Articles of Organization:** Submit this document to your state's Secretary of State office. It typically includes basic information about your business, such as its name, address, and registered agent.

3. **Obtain an EIN (Employer Identification Number):** Apply for an EIN through the IRS website. This number is essential for opening a business bank account and filing taxes.

4. **Open a Business Bank Account:** Separate your personal and business finances by setting up a dedicated account for your publishing company. This simplifies accounting and ensures compliance with tax regulations.

5. **Research State-Specific Requirements:** Some states may require additional steps, such as publishing a notice of formation in a local newspaper or obtaining specific licenses.

Expanding Beyond Self-Publishing

Once your business is established, consider offering publishing services to other authors. This could include editing, design, and distribution services, allowing you to generate additional revenue streams while building your reputation as a publisher. Networking with other authors and attending industry events can help you attract clients and establish your brand in the publishing world.

Publishing books doesn't just open the door to sharing your story—it can also lead to new opportunities to earn money. While creating your book, you may discover a passion for something like formatting or book cover design. If you enjoyed these creative aspects, you can offer them as services to other authors. For example:

- **Book Formatting**: $50–$500, depending on complexity and print vs. eBook. I was recently quoted $8/page. That's $2000 for a 250 page book. Although I don't think I would charge that much, it would be considered the high end of the spectrum.

- **Book Cover Design**: $100–$1,000+, based on experience and custom vs. pre-made covers. You can also hire a designer you trust and be the go-between for your author because they may not know what they really need.

- **Editing Services**: $200–$2,000+, depending on the level of editing (proofreading, copyediting, developmental). Developmental copyediting could get up to $10,000 maybe more depending on cost per page, word or hour.

- **Marketing Assistance**: $50–$1,000+ for services like social media promotion or ad management. Remember to quote the author any additional cost for ad spend which they would be responsible for. (ie. Google Ads or Facebook Ads etc.)

- **Author Coaching**: $50–$300 per hour for guidance through the publishing process. You can create bundled packages that include author coaching or use author coaching as an incentive for authors to buy your publishing package.

Another option is to collaborate with a group on a community publishing project. These can be great for fundraising, group storytelling, or other creative endeavors where multiple authors contribute. Not only do these projects build connections, but they also give authors a chance to support one another while sharing the cost and responsibility of publishing.

Hire an Accountant

One of the biggest pitfalls is not having an accountant. If you're running a business, it's crucial to have someone who can handle your taxes—both business and personal. I pay my accountant $1,000 a year, and while that may seem a little high, it's worth it for the peace of mind. I know enough to know that I don't know, and I'm willing to pay for expertise to ensure my deductions are handled properly and everything is done correctly.

It's also important to keep detailed records of all your expenses and income. Make sure everything is categorized properly and accounted for. I remember my first year in this business—my accountant told me, "You need more write-offs; this isn't right." At first, I thought that meant I needed to spend more money, so I put more into marketing. While that wasn't exactly what he meant, it turned out to be the right move for me because reinvesting in my business helped it grow, and I was able to write it off as an expense.

That said, I'm not giving accounting advice—this is just my experience. I strongly recommend finding someone you trust. Don't rely on chain services like H&R Block. Instead, reach out to your local Chamber of Commerce for recommendations on reliable accountants in your area who specialize in small businesses.

Having been in the self-publishing business since 2017, I can say I've made every mistake you can think of, including poor boundaries and not charging my worth. But it was all a learning process and now I know what to do and how to do it like the back of my hand. That's why I teach classes on self publishing. At some point I want everyone to be fearless when it comes to publishing their books. In this information age, it's vital that we use every means possible to convey our insights and wisdom to leave behind for generations to come.

By following these steps, you'll create a solid foundation for your publishing business. In the next chapter, we'll explore effective marketing strategies to promote your books and drive sales.

Reflections

1. What business structure will you choose for your publishing company, and why?

2. How will you track your publishing finances to ensure profitability and compliance?

3. What services could you offer to other authors to diversify your revenue streams?

Checklist

1. Decide on a business structure (LLC, sole proprietorship, etc.) and register with local authorities.

2. Obtain an EIN from the IRS for tax purposes & open a business bank account.

3. Explore additional publishing services to offer authors.

"SELF-PUBLISHING IS A LOVE LETTER TO YOUR FUTURE SELF THAT SAYS, 'I BELIEVED IN US ENOUGH TO MAKE THIS HAPPEN.'"

Unknown

Chapter 11

Marketing Your Book

Marketing is an essential part of the publishing process, as it ensures your book reaches the right audience. A well-executed marketing strategy can boost your book's visibility, drive sales, and establish your brand as an author or publisher. This chapter provides actionable steps to help you market your book effectively.

Preparing for Launch

A successful book launch begins long before the publication date. Start by building anticipation among your target audience. Create a launch plan that outlines key activities, such as social media announcements, email campaigns, and collaborations with influencers in your niche. Engaging your audience early helps build excitement and ensures they are ready to support your book on launch day.

Building an email list is one of the most effective ways to connect with your audience. Use platforms like Mailchimp or ConvertKit to create a landing page where readers can sign up to receive updates about your book. Offer incentives, such as a free chapter or exclusive content, to encourage sign-ups. A strong email list provides a direct channel to your most loyal supporters.

Optimizing Your Book for Amazon

Amazon is one of the largest book marketplaces, making it a critical platform for self-published authors. To maximize your book's discoverability, focus on optimizing its metadata. This includes:

- **Categories and Keywords:** Use tools like Publisher Rocket or KDP Spy to identify rankable categories and high-traffic keywords. Selecting the right categories can make your book more visible to potential readers.

- **Book Description:** Write a compelling book description that highlights the main benefits and unique aspects of your book. Use formatting options, such as bullet points and bold text, to make your description visually appealing.

- **Pricing Strategies:** Set a competitive price for your book based on its genre and comparable titles. Consider offering introductory pricing or promotions to attract early buyers.

Amazon also offers promotional tools, such as Kindle Countdown Deals and Free Book Promotions. Schedule these promotions strategically to boost your book's ranking and reach new readers.

Leveraging Fiverr for Affordable Marketing

Fiverr is a valuable resource for authors looking to outsource marketing tasks. You can find affordable gigs for services like creating social media ads, designing promotional graphics, and running targeted ad campaigns. When choosing a freelancer, review their portfolio and ratings to ensure they align with your needs.

In addition to paid gigs, explore Fiverr for unique marketing ideas, such as book trailers or animated advertisements. These creative assets can help your book stand out in a competitive market.

Encouraging Reviews and Building Credibility

Positive reviews are critical for building credibility and encouraging new readers to purchase your book. Encourage your readers to leave reviews on platforms like Amazon and Goodreads. Consider reaching out to book bloggers or reviewers in your genre, offering them a free copy of your book in exchange for an honest review.

Incentivize reviews from your email list or social media followers by hosting giveaways or offering exclusive content. However, ensure your approach complies with platform policies to avoid penalties.

By implementing these marketing strategies, you'll increase your book's visibility and establish a strong presence in the publishing industry. In the next chapter, we'll discuss post-publication strategies to sustain your book's momentum and build long-term success.

Marketing Budget Worksheet

Use this worksheet to plan and allocate your promotional spending for your book. Divide your budget into categories and estimate costs to ensure your marketing strategy is effective and stays within your financial means.

1. Total Marketing Budget

- **Total Budget Amount:** $

2. Budget Categories

2.1 Advertising

Allocate funds for paid advertising campaigns to boost visibility and sales.

- **Amazon Ads:** $
- **Facebook Ads:** $
- **BookBub Ads:** $
- **Google Ads:** $
- **Other Platforms (e.g., Instagram):** $

Total Advertising Budget: $

2.2 Professional Services

Consider hiring experts to enhance the quality and reach of your marketing.

- **Marketing Consultant:** $
- **Social Media Manager:** $

- **Publicist:** $

- **Graphic Designer for Ads/Promos:** $

Total Professional Services Budget: $

2.3 Giveaways and Promotions

Plan for free or discounted book promotions to generate interest.

- **Giveaway Prizes (e.g., gift cards, signed copies):** $

- **Platform Fees (e.g., Goodreads Giveaways):** $

- **Discount Campaigns:** $

Total Giveaways and Promotions Budget: $

2.4 Content Creation

Create high-quality content to engage readers and promote your book.

- **Book Trailer Creation:** $

- **Blog Posts or Articles:** $

- **Social Media Content:** $

- **Email Campaigns:** $

Total Content Creation Budget: $

2.5 Influencer Marketing

Collaborate with influencers, bloggers, and reviewers to expand your reach.

- **Review Copies:** $
- **Influencer Fees:** $
- **Sponsored Posts:** $

Total Influencer Marketing Budget: $

2.6 Event Marketing

Plan for virtual or in-person events to connect with readers and promote your book.

- **Virtual Event Hosting Fees:** $
- **Book Signing Events:** $
- **Travel Costs:** $

Total Event Marketing Budget: $

3. Budget Summary

4. Notes and Adjustments

Use this worksheet to evaluate and adjust your marketing efforts as needed. Regularly review your spending to ensure your budget aligns with your promotional goals and results.

Primary Pitfall: Not Marketing Your Book

The biggest pitfall when it comes to marketing your book is simply not doing it. This includes missing opportunities like:

- Pre-sales

- Book signings and sending out copies

- Promoting on social media

- Hosting book readings

- Turning your book into other forms of intellectual property, like classes, younger editions for kids, animations, or YouTube content

Sometimes, authors are so exhausted from writing and publishing their book that they forget to tell people about it—or they feel shy about promoting it. I've been there myself. Someone tells you they're reading your book, and you think, *Oh no, what if it's not good?* But then you remember: *Of course it's good!*

It's okay to get feedback. Not everyone will love your book, and that's fine. What matters is connecting with the people who *do* resonate with it. These are your champions—the readers who will spread the word, recommend your book, and help grow your audience.

Actionable Tips for Marketing

- Engage with your readers. Ask if they belong to book clubs or know of places to recommend your book.

- Host readings or Q&A sessions. These can be in person or virtual on platforms like YouTube.

- Explore creative extensions of your book, like adaptations for younger readers or animations.

- Make your book accessible and easy to find. The more people know about it, the more successful it will be.

The key is to *actually market your book*. Don't let it sit on the shelf. Get it out there, talk about it, and celebrate what you've created.

Hiring a Marketing and Branding Agency can be great just remember that Return on Investment may be low and there are rarely any guarantees.

PR and Marketing Made Simple

You don't need a PR firm to promote your book successfully. With the right strategies and tools, you can take charge of your publicity without spending a fortune. Selling wholesale to retailers is one of the most profitable ways to market your book. Use it as a tool to bundle with services, attract opportunities like podcast interviews and speaking engagements, and promote your other products or solutions through strategic calls to action within the book. Bundling your book with services or solutions adds value and can significantly increase your profit margins.

Presales are a fun and effective way to generate excitement and profits before your book's official release. A simple option is to use KDP's author account to send books directly to readers. For example, if your book sells for $14 and costs $7 (including shipping and tax), you'll make a $7 profit per book. For a more premium experience, you can order wholesale books (around $4 per copy) and create customized packages. Include extras like signed copies, bookmarks, pens, handwritten notes, or even stickers. Wrapping them beautifully and selling them for $25 or more not only delights your audience but also boosts your profits. You can even bundle a signed book with a session or other services to add more value.

Press releases are a powerful tool to announce your book at key milestones, such as the start of presales, the official release, launch parties, bestseller achievements, and podcast appearances. Free press release websites are great for creating visibility and boosting your book's SEO. If you want a more professional touch, Fiverr offers affordable press release distribution services. You can even write your own press release using tools like ChatGPT and have it polished and distributed professionally.

While Amazon is a popular platform for selling books, it's also highly competitive, making it difficult to stand out without significant advertising spend. Many marketing companies promise results, but they often leave authors footing expensive ad bills without seeing much return. Instead, focus on strategies that are more organic, like leveraging your book to secure interviews, speaking opportunities, and local events. These methods build authentic connections and often yield better results than paid ads.

Presales and bonuses don't have to stop once your book is launched. You can continue offering signed copies, exclusive sessions, or free resources to keep your audience engaged and drive ongoing sales. Be sure to update your website regularly to reflect your latest offers.

Finally, remember that learning and adapting is part of the process. Explore different tactics to see what works best for you. For inspiration and tips, check out Bethany Atazadeh's YouTube channel, https://www.youtube.com/@BethanyAtazadeh which is packed with advice on self-promotion. With these strategies, you can confidently handle your PR and marketing while keeping full control of your budget and brand.

If you feel like you want to pursue a marketing and branding agency here is a guide to help you evaluate if it's right for you.

Step-by-Step Guide to Evaluate a Marketing and Branding Agency for Book Publishing

When deciding whether to partner with a marketing and branding agency for publishing your book, it's essential to thoroughly evaluate their offerings and align them with your goals. Here's a step-by-step guide:

1. Clarify Your Goals

- What do you want to achieve? Increased sales, brand visibility, or a professionally polished book?
- Are you looking for a Done-For-You (DFY) solution, or do you prefer to learn and handle

marketing yourself?

- Set clear expectations about ROI, time commitment, and deliverables.

2. Analyze Their Offerings

- Review the services they provide, some things you may be able to do on you own. Look for specifics like:

  ○ Keyword Research: You can DIY this by using Publisher Rocket. https://publisherrocket.com/

  ○ BISAC Category Implementation: You can DIY this by using Publisher Rocket. https://publisherrocket.com/

  ○ Book Descriptions and Author Bios: You can get your book description from ChatGPT as well as your author bio.

  ○ Social Media and Marketing Strategies: If you already have a good following putting your book out there yourself can be fun and easy. Otherwise, you can join large Facebook Book Groups that allow you to promote your books for free. You can also connect with other authors and work as a team to promote each others books and get reviews.

- Amazon Ads and Book Promotional Ads: Remember you are responsible for paying for the ads to get out or Ad Spend even if they make the images or ads for you.

- Website Design and Branding Packages: You will still be responsible for paying for your website but they may design it for you and have a cohesive brand imaging, colors and fonts. If that's something you don't feel confident in, then it would make sense to use an outside agency for help.

- A+ Content for Amazon: You can do this but may want to hire a designer for the book banner images, author bio images etc.

- Compare their services to what you already have or can do yourself.

3. Investigate Their Reputation

- Research online reviews, testimonials, and case studies.

- Check their social media presence and look for any red flags or negative feedback.

- Visit their website and explore their library of previous projects to assess quality and consistency.

4. Ask Detailed Questions

- **About Ads:**
  - Do they create ads and choose appropriate keywords?
  - Where will the ads be placed (Amazon, Google, etc.)?
  - What is the typical ROI vs. ad spend over 3-6 months?
  - Are you responsible for ad spend, and is it included in their fee structure?

- **About Strategy:**
  - What's included in their marketing and social media strategy?
  - Is the strategy actionable, or will they implement it for you?

- **About Branding:**
  - What's included in the branding package?

(Logo, visuals, messaging, etc.)

- Can they provide examples of branding work they've done for other authors?

- **About Websites:**

    - Will the website include SEO optimization?

    - What's their plan for driving traffic to the site?

    - Are there additional costs (e.g., hosting, domain registration)?

5. Review Their Library

- Visit their website and look for a portfolio or library of books they've worked on.

- Check if the books have A+ Content or other features that make them stand out on platforms like Amazon.

- Spot-check the authors they've worked with to see if their branding and websites are visible and effective.

6. Evaluate Pricing and ROI

- Ask for a detailed breakdown of their fees.

- Inquire about potential hidden costs (e.g., ad spend, hosting fees).

- Evaluate the potential ROI—both in terms of revenue and brand visibility.

7. Weigh the Pros and Cons

- Assess what they offer versus what you already have or can do on your own.

- Determine whether their expertise justifies the cost.

- Consider whether their services align with your short-term and long-term goals.

8. Make an Informed Decision

- If their offerings fill critical gaps in your strategy, they might be a good fit.

- If you already have most of the tools and strategies they offer, consider handling those elements yourself.

- Remember, no agency can guarantee high royalties or consistent book sales—your involvement and creativity are crucial.

By following these steps, you'll have a clearer picture of whether a marketing and branding agency is the right fit for your publishing journey. Don't hesitate to dig deep into their offerings and track record before making a decision!

Reflections

1. Who is your target audience, and how will you tailor your marketing efforts to reach them?

2. Which marketing channels (e.g., email, social media, ads) will you prioritize, and why?

3. How will you encourage readers to leave reviews and build credibility for your book?

Checklist

1. Build an email list with tools like Mailchimp or ConvertKit.

2. Optimize your book metadata for discoverability.

3. Use tools like Publisher Rocket to select categories and keywords.

4. Plan a promotional strategy, including discounts or free promotions.

5. Hire freelancers for marketing support via Fiverr.

6. Encourage reviews by engaging readers and influencers.

7. Schedule ongoing social media and email campaigns.

"SUCCESS IS STUMBLING FROM FAILURE TO FAILURE WITH NO LOSS OF ENTHUSIASM."

Winston Churchill

Chapter 12

Post-Publication Strategies

Publishing your book is only the beginning of your journey as an author or publisher. After the initial launch excitement fades, it's important to implement strategies that keep your book relevant and maintain its momentum. This chapter explores ways to monitor performance, expand your reach, and reinvest in your success.

Monitoring Book Performance and Sales

Tracking the performance of your book helps you understand what works and what doesn't. Most publishing platforms, like KDP, IngramSpark, and Draft2Digital, offer analytics tools that provide valuable insights into sales trends, reader demographics, and geographic distribution.

- **Key Metrics to Monitor:**
    - Sales volume and revenue over time.
    - Reader reviews and ratings.
    - Category rankings on platforms like Amazon.
- **Using Analytics for Decision-Making:** Analyze your book's performance to identify areas for improvement. For instance, if sales drop after the launch, it might indicate a need for renewed marketing efforts or pricing adjustments. Use reader feedback to guide potential updates or corrections to your book.

Expanding Distribution Channels

As your book gains traction, consider broadening its availability to reach new audiences. If you started with a single platform, such as KDP, explore additional distribution options like IngramSpark for print-on-demand or Draft2Digital for expanded eBook reach. Libraries and independent bookstores are excellent channels for connecting with dedicated readers.

- **Maximizing International Reach:** Many platforms offer global distribution options, allowing you to tap into international markets. Tailor your marketing efforts to target these audiences effectively.

- **Creating Bundles or Special Editions:** Combine multiple titles or create limited-edition versions to appeal to dedicated fans and collectors.

Reinvesting Profits into Marketing

Reinvesting a portion of your book's earnings back into marketing is essential for sustained growth. Allocate funds for advertising on platforms like Google Ads or BookBub. Experiment with different ad types and audiences to determine what generates the best return on investment.

- **Collaborating with Influencers:** Partner with bloggers, podcasters, or social media influencers in your genre to promote your book. These collaborations can introduce your work to a broader audience.

- **Hosting Virtual or In-Person Events:** Organize book readings, webinars, or signings to engage with your readers and build a community around your work.

Creating a Long-Term Marketing Plan

Developing a consistent marketing strategy ensures your book remains relevant in the long run. Schedule periodic promotions, such as seasonal discounts or anniversary celebrations. Stay active on social media and continue engaging with your audience to maintain interest.

By implementing these post-publication strategies, you'll maximize your book's potential and lay the groundwork for future projects. In the next chapter, we'll discuss how to build a long-term publishing career and scale your efforts for sustained success.

Post-Production Strategies

This one is simple: just get in there and stay engaged with your publishing platforms. I suggest regularly logging into your KDP or IngramSpark account—ideally every two weeks, but at least once a month.

Multiple Accounts

If you didn't know, you can have more than one KDP account. For example, we have an account for *As You Wish Publishing* and another for *As You Wish Publishing Classics*. You can have multiple accounts and use the same tax ID number for all of them.

Stay Active

When you log in, make a habit of ordering a book and sending it to yourself. This keeps some energy in your account and ensures everything is working as it should. Whether you're actively working on a book or just checking sales, staying engaged helps you keep the momentum going.

Also, watch for announcements from KDP or IngramSpark. These platforms often post updates at the top of their dashboards, like requests to update your tax information. If you don't update this information when requested, they won't pay your royalties. When you first set up your account, you'll input your tax and legal information, but occasionally, they'll ask for updates. Staying on top of this ensures you get paid on time.

Order Copies

In addition to monitoring sales, I recommend buying a copy of your book directly from Amazon now and then. Also, keep some author copies on hand for events, friends, or giveaways. You never know when you'll want to share your book!

There's something empowering about handing someone a physical copy of your work. Some authors even keep books in the back of their car to give away or sell on the spot. You can sell them for $10, sign them, and make a moment of it. It's a very grassroots, organic approach that can feel incredibly rewarding.

In Summary

Ultimately, just stay involved. Regularly check your accounts, order books, make sure your information is up to date, and keep the energy flowing. It's a simple way to ensure everything is running smoothly and to stay connected to your work.

Reflections

1. What metrics will you track to evaluate your book's performance over time?

2. How will you expand your distribution channels to reach a wider audience?

3. What percentage of your royalties will you reinvest in marketing or future projects?

Checklist

1. Monitor book performance using analytics tools.

2. Expand distribution channels as your book gains traction.

3. Reinvest royalties into marketing efforts.

4. Explore bundling books or creating special editions.

5. Cross-promote with other authors.

"DON'T BE AFRAID OF BEING SEEN TRYING. THE WORLD NEEDS MORE PEOPLE BRAVE ENOUGH TO SHARE THEIR WORK."

Unknown

Chapter 13

Long-Term Success in Publishing

Building a successful publishing career involves more than just publishing one book—it requires planning, adaptation, and continuous improvement. In this final chapter, we'll explore strategies for scaling your publishing efforts, networking in the industry, and staying ahead of trends.

Long-term publishing is all about creating avenues and funnels that help people connect with you. Building your brand as an author is so important. This could mean writing multiple books or taking one book and creating new opportunities from it—whether it's a course, a game, a young readers' version, or a teen adaptation. Think about the direction you want to take and how you can expand on your existing work.

Branding Your Books

As you grow your catalog, consider branding your books with a cohesive look—similar colors, fonts, or layouts. For example, think of the *Chicken Soup for the Soul* series. No matter which book in the series you pick up—whether it's *Chicken Soup for the Horse Lover's Soul* or *Chicken Soup for the Mother's Soul*—they all have the same recognizable fonts, layouts, and overall design. That consistency makes the brand immediately identifiable.

At *As You Wish Publishing*, we've approached things a bit differently. While all of our books fall under the self-help category, some are more "woo-woo," while others are more science-based. Our covers, fonts, colors, and images vary widely, so you wouldn't necessarily recognize them as part of a cohesive brand. That's something I've been thinking about a lot.

For our new classics line (public domain books we're publishing), I'm taking a more consistent approach. Each book will have the same basic layout and fonts, with a tag on the front that includes the book title, the original author, and "edited by" credits. The cover image will match the theme or energy of the book. For example, *The I AM Discourses* features a violet flame on the cover, while *The Tao Te Ching* has a serene, light, Asian-inspired landscape. This cohesive design creates a clear identity for the series.

If you know you'll be publishing a series or books under a single theme, I highly recommend planning your branding strategy. It can help readers recognize and connect with your work, making your books stand out.

Networking and Community

Long-term success also involves connecting with other authors and staying active in the community. Look into events like Author Nation's self-publishing annual event or Self-Publishing Princess. These are great places to learn, network, and share your experiences.

That said, be mindful of online spaces like Facebook or other social media platforms. While they can be useful, they're also full of naysayers—people who may not fully understand publishing and might discourage others with negativity or unrelated arguments about things like vanity presses. Ignore the noise. Focus on learning the skills and processes you need to publish your book effectively.

Your First Book Is Just the Beginning

Think of your first book as a test run—a chance to learn and grow. Use it as an educational tool. If you do well with that book, write another one. And another. Writing and publishing can become a joyful process, like any other creative hobby. Some people spend hours crocheting or fixing cars; maybe your thing is writing books and sharing them with the world.

Every page, chapter, and book you write builds your platform as an author. Embrace that identity and keep moving forward.

Building a Brand as an Author or Publisher

Establishing a strong personal or company brand is essential for long-term success. Your brand reflects your values, voice, and the promise you make to your audience. Start by defining your unique selling proposition (USP)—what sets you apart from other authors or publishers?

- **Consistency Across Platforms:** Use consistent messaging, visuals, and tone across your website, social media profiles, and marketing materials. A cohesive brand builds trust and recognition among readers.

- **Engaging with Your Audience:** Foster a loyal community by regularly interacting with your readers. Share updates, behind-the-scenes content, and exclusive offers to deepen their connection with your work.

Scaling Up with Multiple Books

Publishing multiple books is one of the most effective ways to grow your career. Each new title builds on the momentum of your previous works, attracting more readers and increasing your revenue streams.

- **Series and Spin-Offs**: Writing a series or spin-off allows you to capitalize on an existing audience while expanding your universe. This strategy works particularly well in genres like fantasy, romance, and thriller.

- **Batch Writing and Planning**: Plan and write multiple books simultaneously to streamline your workflow. Tools like Trello or Scrivener can help you manage complex projects efficiently.

Networking with Other Authors and Publishers

Building relationships within the publishing community can lead to valuable collaborations and opportunities. Attend industry events, join online forums, and participate in author groups to connect with like-minded professionals.

- **Collaborative Marketing Efforts**: Partner with other authors to co-host events, bundle books, or cross-promote each other's work. These initiatives can expand your reach and introduce you to new audiences.

- **Learning from Peers:** Stay open to feedback and advice from experienced authors and publishers. Their insights can help you navigate challenges and refine your approach.

Staying Updated on Industry Trends

The publishing industry is constantly evolving, with new tools, platforms, and reader preferences shaping the landscape. Staying informed ensures you remain competitive and adaptable.

- **Subscribe to Industry Newsletters:** Follow reputable sources like Publishers Weekly, The Creative Penn, and Jane Friedman for updates and insights.

- **Experiment with Emerging Formats:** Explore opportunities in formats like audiobooks, interactive eBooks, or serialized content to stay ahead of the curve.

The publishing world is constantly evolving, and staying updated on industry trends can help you succeed. For example, when I first started, I hand-formatted a large, oddly dimensioned book in Word—a laborious process. Today, tools like Atticus streamline formatting and save so much time. If I hadn't kept up with advancements, I'd never be able to manage the workload I have now.

As technology like AI continues to grow, it will make certain parts of publishing easier and allow you to focus on the creative aspects—which is the heart of it all. Staying informed and adaptable will help you thrive in the long term.

Publishing Roadmap Worksheet

Use this worksheet to plan and track your publishing journey. Fill out each section to create a detailed roadmap for your book project.

1. Book Information

- **Book Title:**
- **Subtitle:**
- **Author Name:**
- **Genre/Category:**

- **Target Audience:**
- **Anticipated Word Count:**
- **Estimated Publication Date:**

2. Manuscript Preparation

- **Current Status of Manuscript:**
- **Editing Plan:**
  - Editor(s) to Hire:
  - Self-Editing Tools to Use:
- **Formatting Tools:**
  - Print:
  - eBook:
- **Deadlines:**
  - Editing Completion:
  - Formatting Completion:

3. Publishing Platforms

- **Selected Platforms:**
- **Account Setup Completion:**

- Platform 1:
- Platform 2:

- **ISBN Information:**
  - Number Purchased:
  - Assigned ISBNs:

4. Book Design

- **Cover Design Plan:**
- **Interior Layout Plan:**

5. Marketing Strategy

- **Key Audience Insights:**
  - Who are your readers?
  - What problems or desires does your book address?
- **Marketing Channels:**
- **Budget Allocation:**
  - Editing/Proofreading:
  - Cover Design:

- Advertising:

6. Launch Plan

- **Key Dates:**

  - Pre-Launch Campaign Start:

  - ARC (Advance Review Copy) Distribution:

  - Official Launch Date:

- **Launch Activities:**

7. Post-Launch Actions

- **Performance Metrics to Track:**

  - Sales:

  - Downloads:

  - Reviews:

- **Follow-Up Marketing:**

Notes and Next Steps

Use this roadmap to stay organized and ensure each step of your publishing journey is completed effectively. Regularly update this worksheet to reflect progress and adjust plans as needed.

Reflections

1. How will you develop and maintain a cohesive brand as an author or publisher?

2. What strategies will you use to scale your publishing efforts and grow your catalog?

3. How will you stay informed about industry trends and adapt to changes in the publishing landscape?

Checklist

1. Develop a cohesive personal or imprint brand.

2. Plan and publish multiple books to build your catalog.

3. Network with industry professionals and authors.

4. Stay informed about publishing trends.

5. Experiment with new formats, such as audiobooks or serialized content.

"START WHERE YOU ARE. USE WHAT YOU HAVE. DO WHAT YOU CAN."

Arthur Ashe

Conclusion

Congratulations on completing *Publishing Made Easy*. By now, you should have a clear understanding of the entire publishing process, from preparing your manuscript to creating long-term success as an author or publisher. This guide has equipped you with actionable steps to:

- Polish and format your manuscript to a professional standard.

- Navigate and utilize major publishing platforms like KDP, IngramSpark, and Draft2Digital.

- Market your book effectively to reach your target audience and boost visibility.

- Establish a publishing business or imprint to build a sustainable and credible presence in the industry.

- Create additional opportunities for growth through audiobooks, collaborations, and multiple formats.

Publishing your book is a remarkable achievement, and it's only the beginning of your journey. Whether you aim to write more books, expand your publishing business, or become a recognized name in your genre, the possibilities are endless. Keep learning, experimenting, and engaging with your audience to refine your approach and adapt to the ever-changing publishing landscape.

Remember, the tools and strategies shared in this guide are just the foundation. Your passion, creativity, and determination will ultimately drive your success. Stay connected to your goals, celebrate every milestone, and continue building the publishing career of your dreams.

Here's to your publishing success—happy writing, publishing, and thriving!

Appendices

Glossary of Publishing Terms

1. **ISBN (International Standard Book Number):** A unique identifier for books, essential for retail and library distribution.

2. **Metadata:** Information about your book, including title, author, description, keywords, and categories, used to optimize discoverability.

3. **Trim Size:** The dimensions of your printed book.

4. **Royalties:** The percentage of sales revenue an author earns from their book.

5. **Advance:** A payment made to an author before their book earns royalties.

6. **Preassigned Control Number (PCN):** A Library of Congress number assigned before a book is published.

7. **Proof Copy:** A printed version of your book for review before final publication.

8. **ARC (Advanced Reader Copy):** The PDF copy you will give your review teams and early readers

Checklist for Publishing Your Book

1. Complete manuscript editing and proofreading.

2. Format manuscript for print and digital publication.

3. Design a professional cover.

4. Select publishing platforms (e.g., KDP, IngramSpark, Draft2Digital).

5. Purchase and assign ISBNs.

6. Apply for a Library of Congress Control Number (if applicable).

7. Optimize metadata (keywords, categories, and description).

8. Set pricing and distribution options.

9. Plan and execute a marketing strategy.

10. Launch the book and monitor performance.

Recommended Tools and Resources

1. **Editing and Proofreading:** Grammarly https://www.grammarly.com, ProWritingAid https://prowritingaid.com, Reedsy https://reedsy.com.

2. **Formatting:** Atticus https://www.atticus.io, Vellum https://vellum.pub, Calibre https://calibre-ebook.com.

3. **Cover Design:** Canva https://www.canva.com, Book Brush https://bookbrush.com, Fiverr https://www.fiverr.com.

4. **Publishing Platforms:** Kindle Direct Publishing (https://kdp.amazon.com), IngramSpark https://www.ingramspark.com, Draft2Digital https://draft2digital.com.

5. **Marketing Tools:** Publisher Rocket https://publisherrocket.com, BookBub https://www.bookbub.com, Flodesk https://flodesk.com/c/XWZ7LH (This link gives you %50 off your

monthly fee for email distribution for the 1st 12 months)

6. **Audiobooks:** Audible/ACX https://www.acx.com

7. **Scrivener:** https://scrivener.app/

YouTube Channels

1. Self-Published Author Bethany Atazadeh: https://www.youtube.com/@BethanyAtazadeh

2. Book Launchers: https://www.youtube.com/@BookLaunchers

3. Kindlepreneur: https://www.youtube.com/@Kindlepreneur

4. The Nerdy Novelist: https://www.youtube.com/@TheNerdyNovelist

5. As You Wish Publishing: https://www.youtube.com/@AsYouWishPublishing

6. Book Cover Design: https://www.youtube.com/@bookcoversdiy

Sample Timelines for Publishing and Marketing

1. **Six Months Before Launch:**

   - Complete manuscript editing and initial formatting.

   - Develop a marketing plan and build an email list.

   - Design your book cover.

2. **Three Months Before Launch:**

   - Set up accounts on publishing platforms.

   - Finalize book formatting and metadata.

   - Plan promotional campaigns (e.g., free promotions, ads).

3. **One Month Before Launch:**

   - Order proof copies for review.

   - Start a pre-launch social media campaign.

   - Reach out to reviewers and influencers.

4. **Launch Week:**

   - Announce your book on all platforms.

   - Execute promotional offers.

- Engage with readers and respond to reviews.

5. **Post-Launch:**
    - Monitor sales and analytics.
    - Continue marketing efforts (e.g., ads, collaborations).
    - Plan the next book or project.

PR and Marketing Made Simple

1. Be Your Own PR Person

You don't need to hire a PR firm to succeed in promoting your book. With the right strategies and tools, you can take charge of your publicity effectively and affordably.

Key Takeaway: Leverage your existing skills, utilize affordable tools, and save money without sacrificing results.

2. Focus on Selling Wholesale to Retail

Selling your book wholesale to retailers is one of the most profitable strategies. Use your book as a tool to:

- **Bundle with services:** Offer your book alongside coaching, consulting, or other services.

- **Attract opportunities:** Use your book as a gateway to podcast interviews, speaking engagements, and collaborations.

- **Promote products/solutions:** Drive readers to your other products or solutions through strategic calls to action inside the book.

Tip: Bundling services with your book adds value and increases profit margins.

3. Run Effective Presales

Presales can be both fun and profitable. Here are two proven strategies:

1. **Basic Option:**

   - Use KDP's author account to send books directly to readers.

   - Example: If your book costs $14, your cost is about $7 (including shipping/tax), leaving you with a $7 profit margin per sale.

2. **Premium Option:**

   - Order wholesale books (around $4 per copy) and create a customized package.

   - Add extras: Signed copies, bookmarks, pens,

handwritten notes, stickers, and gift wrapping.

- Charge $25+ per copy.

Profit Breakdown:

For a $25 premium package:

- $4 (book) + $6 (shipping) = $10 cost.

- $15+ profit per book.

Bonus Tip: Offer bundle deals (e.g., signed book + coaching session) to maximize value.

4. Leverage Press Releases

Press releases are a powerful way to gain visibility and credibility. Here's how to maximize them:

- **Key Milestones for Press Releases:**

    - Announce upcoming book presales.

    - Celebrate the official book release.

    - Promote launch parties or free download events.

    - Highlight bestseller status.

    - Announce podcast appearances, local book

tours, and other media features.

- **Where to Submit Press Releases:**
  - Use free press release websites for basic announcements (great for SEO and "Google juice").
  - Explore Fiverr gigs for professional distribution at affordable prices.

DIY Tip: Use AI tools like ChatGPT to craft professional press releases tailored to your announcements.

5. Avoid Common Marketing Pitfalls

- **Be wary of expensive ad campaigns**: Many marketing companies charge high fees for ads with little to no ROI.
- **Focus on organic growth strategies**: Building authentic connections through podcasts, interviews, and speaking engagements is often more effective.

Reality Check: Selling on platforms like Amazon can be challenging due to high competition and advertising costs. Instead, focus on strategies that give you control over your sales and profit margins.

6. Learn and Adapt

- Experiment with different PR and marketing tactics to find what resonates with your audience.

- For inspiration, check out Bethany Atazadeh's YouTube channel for actionable tips on self-promotion.

7. Build Buzz with Bonus Offers

Even after your presale phase ends, you can continue offering bonuses like signed copies, exclusive sessions, or free resources to keep driving sales.

Pro Tip: Update your website regularly to reflect current offers and promotions.

By following these steps, you can confidently manage your PR and marketing efforts, maximize your book's potential, and build lasting connections with your audience. Remember, you're more than capable of achieving these results on your own!

About the Author

Kyra Schaefer, the Co-Founder and CEO of As You Wish Publishing, a venture established with her husband, Todd Schaefer, since 2017 she has dedicated herself to empowering individuals to illuminate their unique essence and share their narratives with the world. Leading As You Wish Publishing, Kyra spearheads the publication of solo and collaborative books, available in both print and ebook formats. She is also committed to educating authors through her Publishing Made Easy Classes and YouTube Channel. She insists that publishing is for anyone with a dream of creating a book, not just a select few.

The diverse array of books produced by As You Wish Publishing, whether authored individually or through collaboration, cover a broad spectrum of topics such as self-discovery, personal journeys, healing, holistic business, therapeutic modalities, coaching, and spirituality. Kyra, alongside her husband, has successfully collaborated with hundreds of authors, embracing a variety of ages, writing styles, and creative approaches.

Beyond her role as a bestselling author, renowned for "Holograms and Echoes: Transform Triggers to Truth," Kyra Schaefer's passion extends to creating empowering, joyful, and insightful writing and publishing classes tailored for small groups.

Her expertise also spans certifications in Positive Psychology, Art Therapy, and as a Master Practitioner in Neurolinguistics and Hypnosis. With a rich career spanning two decades, Kyra has positively impacted thousands of clients in her role as an emotional therapy practitioner.

ABOUT THE AUTHOR

Reach Kyra at connect@asyouwishpublishing.com and www.asyouwishpublishing.com